Living in a Rain Forest

By Allan Fowler

Consultant
Linda Cornwell, Coordinator of School Quality
and Professional Improvement
Indiana State Teachers Association

Children's Press®
A Division of Grolier Publishing
New York   London   Hong Kong   Sydney
Danbury, Connecticut

Visit Children's Press® on the Internet at:
http://publishing.grolier.com

Designer: Herman Adler Design Group

Library of Congress Cataloging-in-Publication Data

Fowler, Allan.
    Living in a rain forest / by Allan Fowler; consultant, Linda Cornwell.
       p.   cm.   —   (Rookie read-about geography)
    Includes index.
    Summary: Describes the ecology of the rain forest; and the daily life,
dwellings, and food habits of tribes living in the region.
       ISBN: 0-516-21555-8 (lib. bdg.)   0-516-27050-8 (pbk.)
    1. Rain forest people Juvenile literature. 2. Rain forests Juvenile
literature. 3. Rain forest ecology Juvenile literature. [1. Rain forest
people. 2. Rain forests. 3. Rain forest ecology. 4. Ecology.]
    I. Title.   II. Series.
GN394.F68   2000
333.75—dc21   99-14944
                                                                  CIP

Does this look like a good
place to live? It is a tropical
rain forest.

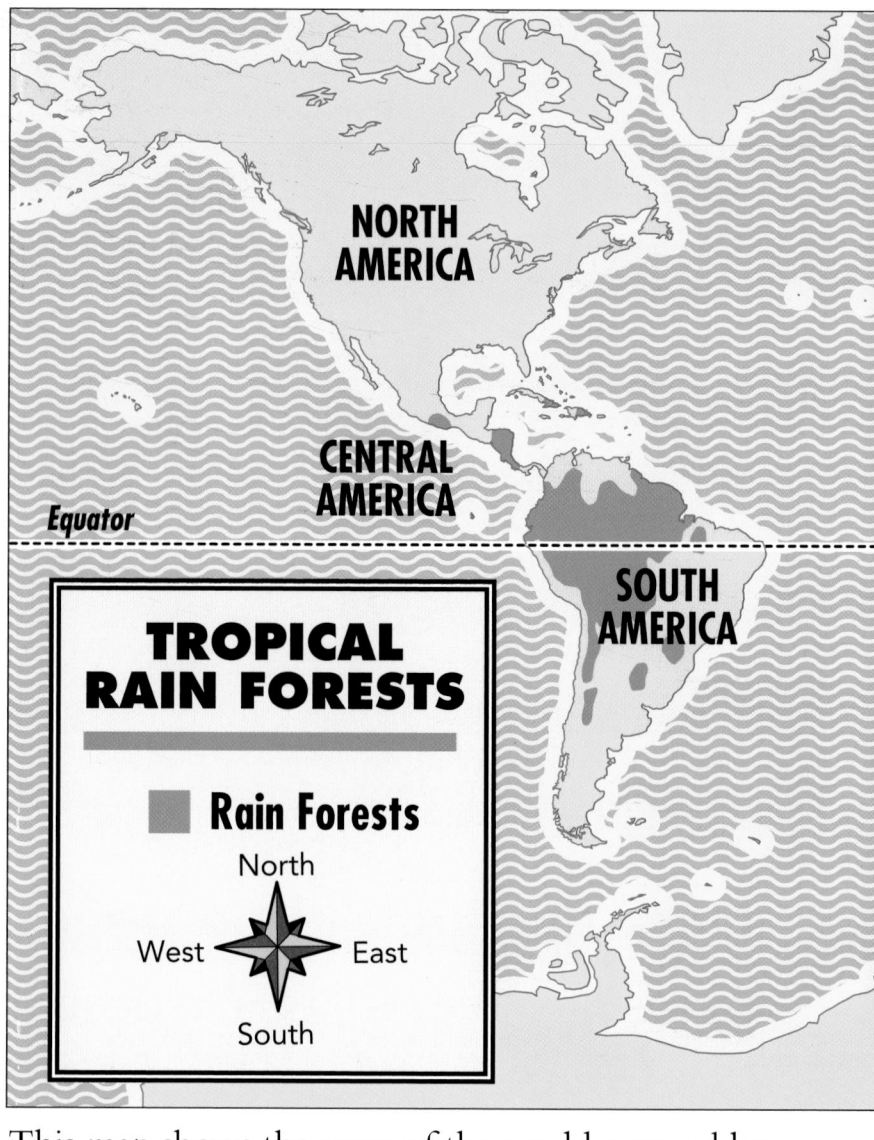

This map shows the areas of the world covered by rain forest.

4

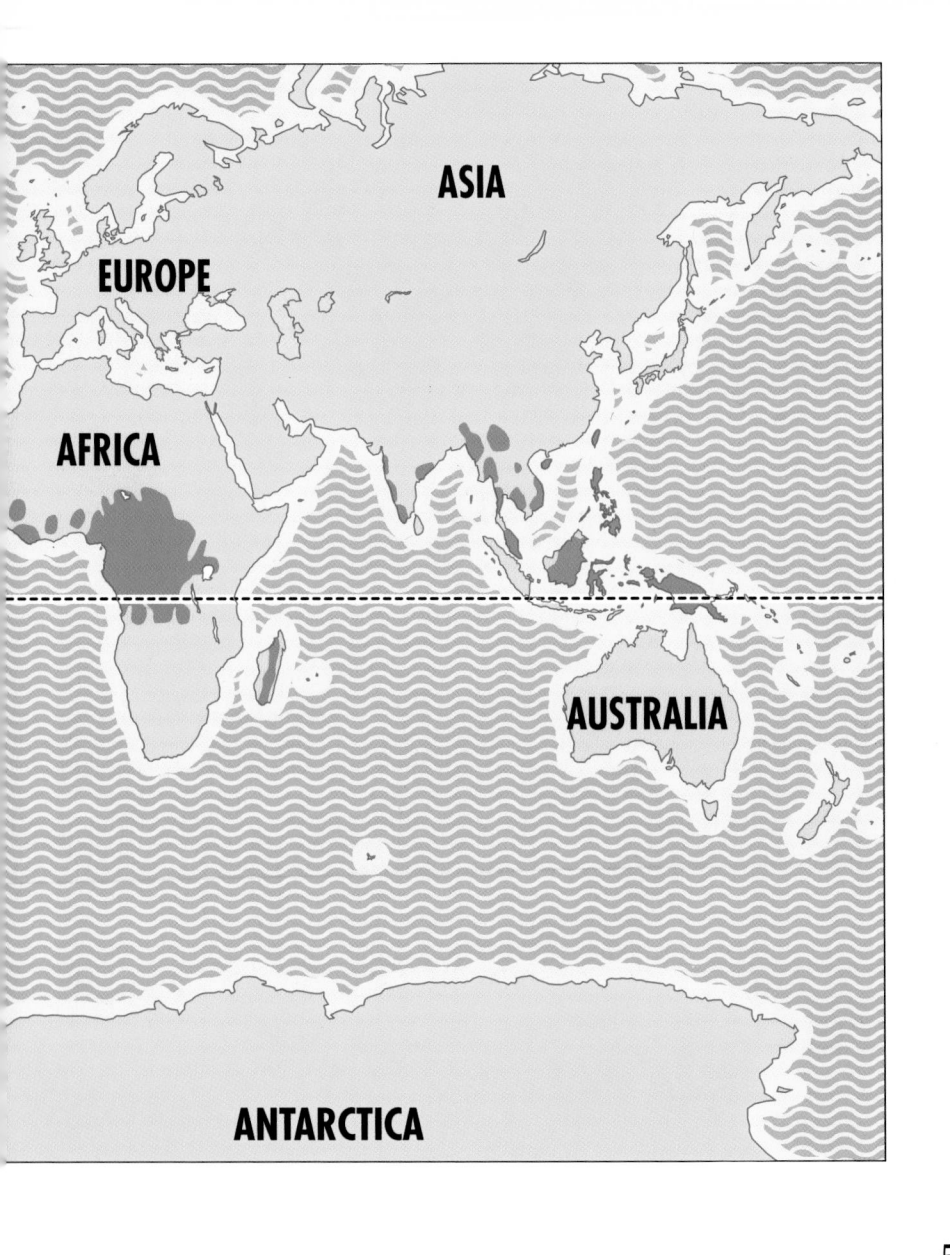

ASIA

EUROPE

AFRICA

AUSTRALIA

ANTARCTICA

5

A rainbow shines over this rain forest canopy.

Tropical rain forests are found in very warm parts of the world. The trees there grow close together.

The leaves form a sort of roof high above the ground. This roof is called a canopy.

Imagine standing in a rain forest. You would hardly be able to see the sky or the sun. The canopy blocks them out.

You probably would get wet, too. It rains almost every day in a rain forest.

A rain forest tribe

Rain forests are full of plant and animal life, but not much human life.

Some people do make their homes in rain forests. They live in groups called tribes.

The tribes have a way of life that is much different from what you may be used to. They have no electricity, no refrigerators, no televisions, and no cars.

People living in a rain forest often use canoes to travel.

Traveling by canoe

Thatched huts

Rain forest houses are thatched huts. "Thatched" means made from reeds, straw, or leaves.

A rain forest tribe might build its huts along a river. There the people can catch fish. They might hunt small animals, such as monkeys, to eat.

A rain forest hunter

Cassava roots

18

Rain forest people also eat plants. Some Indians of the Amazon rain forest make their food from the roots of a plant called cassava (kuh-SAH-vuh).

The Amazon rain forest is found in South America. It is the largest rain forest in the world.

Many interesting animals and birds are found in the Amazon rain forest. This bird is called a toucan (TOO-kan).

Toucan

21

Leopards live in the rain forest of Africa.

Much of central Africa is rain forest. There are also tropical rain forests in southeastern Asia.

The trees of a rain forest
are some of the oldest
and tallest in the world.

This rain forest tree is so
tall, the top of it can't even
be seen in this picture.

A rain forest area cleared of trees

rain forest

thatched hut

toucan

tribe

31

Index

Africa, 22, 23
Amazon rain forest, 19, 20
animals, 16, 20
Asia, 23
birds, 20
canoes, 12, 13
canopy, 6, 7, 8
cassava, 18, 19
farms, 27
Indians, 19
leopards, 22
plant life, 11, 19

rain forest 3, 4–5, 7, 8, 10–12,
   20, 23, 24, 27, 28
rain, 8
river, 16
roads, 27
South America, 20
thatched huts, 14, 15, 16
toucan, 20, 21
towns, 27
trees, 7, 24, 25
tribes, 10, 11, 12

About the Author

Allan Fowler is a freelance writer with a background in advertising.
Born in New York, he now lives in Chicago and enjoys traveling.

Photo Credits

©: Kevin Schafer: 6, 9, 21, 30 top, 31 top left, 31 bottom left; Peter Arnold Inc.:
10, 17, 31 bottom right (BIOS/A. Compost), 22, 30 bottom right (BIOS/
Dennis-Huott), 13 (Brecelj & Hodalic/Still Pictures); Photo Researchers: 18, 30
bottom left (G. Buttner/Naturbild/OKAPIA); Tony Stone Images: 3 (Hans
Strand), Victor Englebert: 25, 26, 29; Visuals Unlimited: cover (Francis E.
Caldwell), 14, 31 top right (Inga Spence).

Map by Joe LeMonnier.

Tropical rain forests are being cut down every day.

Roads, towns, and farms now stand where rain forests once were.

But most rain forests are protected from being completely cut down.

The people of the rain forests will continue to live there for many years.

Words You Know

canopy

cassava root

leopard